Bobby the Blue Elephant

Written by

Duane Hauser

By the Candlelight Publishing

Author's Note

My hopes for writing this book is for you to have many days of interaction and fun learning with your children.

Every Elephant
you have probably
seen is GREY...

An Elephant might smash something if he touches it…

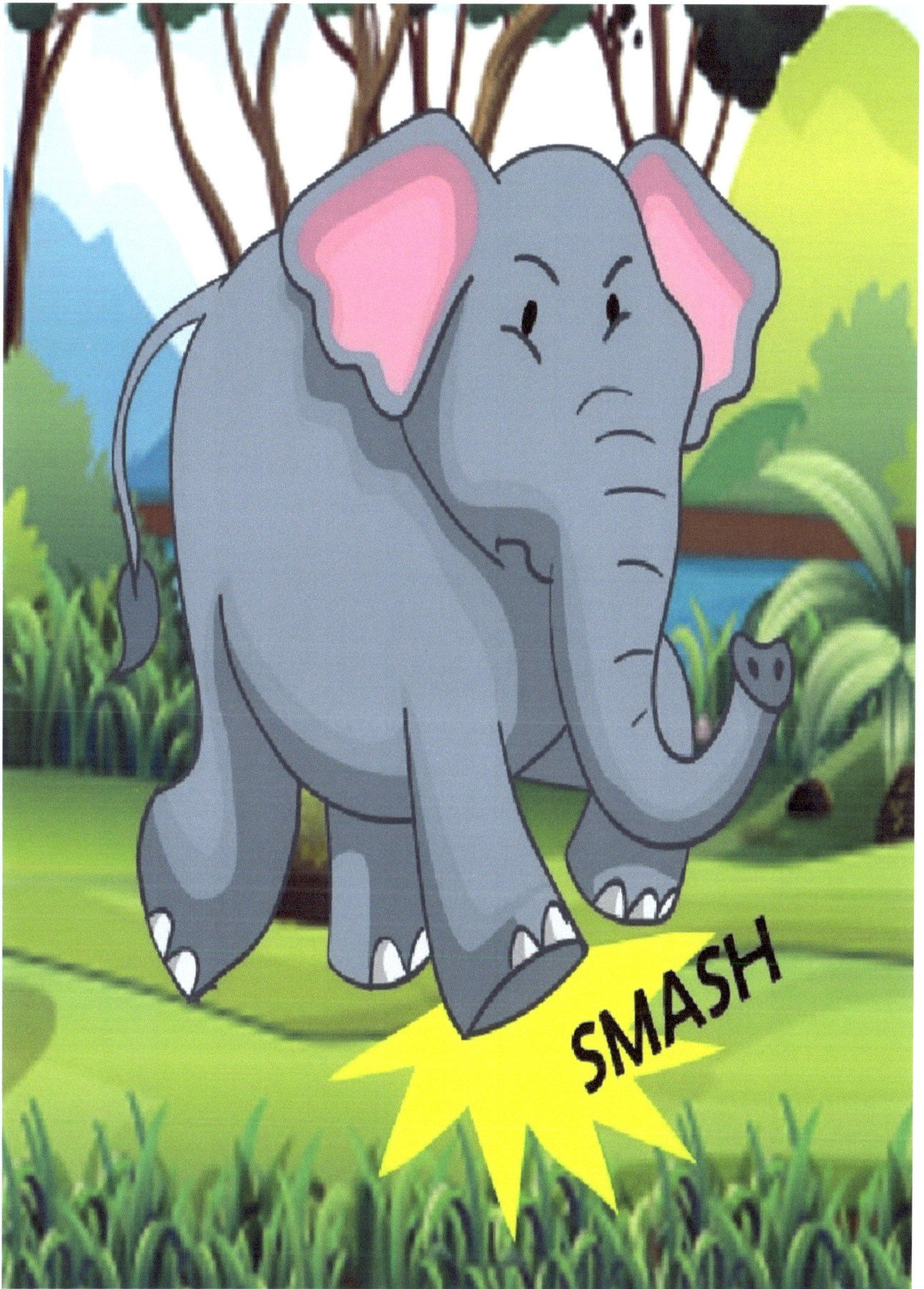

He could never change the color.

If he touches a

YELLOW

pear...

It stays YELLOW

This is the story of Bobby the BLUE elephant. He looks just like other elephants, except...

He is BLUE!

There is one
more thing…

When Bobby touches something, it turns BLUE!

Strawberries are

RED...

When Bobby touches them, they will turn...

BLUE!

Bananas are

YELLOW...

When Bobby touches them, they will turn. . .

BLUE!

Oranges are Orange...

When Bobby
touches them,
they will turn…

BLUE!

Peas are

GREEN...

When Bobby touches them, they will turn…

BLUE!

But when Bobby

touches a

Blueberry…

It stays BLUE!

Bobby only

turns things…

BLUE!

Be careful not to
let Bobby touch
you…

Or you will

turn...

BLUE!

www.ingramcontent.com/pod-product-compliance
Lightning Source LLC
Chambersburg PA
CBHW042101040426
42448CB00002B/99